609 LETTER TEMPLATE AND CREDIT REPAIR SECRETS

How To File A Credit Dispute And Increase Your Score. The Ultimate Guide To Everything You Must Know, With Sample Letters To Defend Your Rights.

Author: **Tony Risk**

Table Of Contents

Introduction

One of the most important topics when it comes to credit card debt is known as the secret way to get out of credit card debt, or section 609. Its name comes from what section it is under the Fair Credit Reporting Act. A 609 is known as a dispute letter, which you would send to your creditor if you saw you were overcharged or unfairly charged. Most people use a 609 message to get the information they feel they should have received. There are several reasons why some information might be kept from you. However, most of it falls under the category of the credit card company trying to scam you out of more money. Initially, being a careful one would be the best thing for you to do.

Take a moment to think about how closely you look over your credit card bill or any of the terms of service of information sent by your credit card company. If you are similar to everyone else, you rarely look too closely. Itis how credit card companies' scam their customers out of money; they know people don't always pay close attention.

The 609 letters can quickly help you delete your bad credit. Other than this, there are a couple of other benefits you will receive from the message. One of these benefits is that you will obtain your documentation and information as the credit bureau has to release this information to you. Secondly, you will be able to get an accurate credit report, which can help you increase your credit score.

There are also disadvantages to the 609 letters. One of these disadvantages is that collection agencies can add information to your credit history at any time. A second disadvantage is that you still have to repay debt. You cannot use the 609 letters to remove debt that you are obligated to pay. Finally, your creditor can do their investigation and add the information back into your credit report, even if it was removed (Irby, 2019).

One of the reasons section 609 came to be is because one of five people state they have inaccurate information on the credit report (Black, 2019). At the same time, many people believe that this statistic is higher than 20 percent of Americans. There are various reasons for this, such as the fact that some people don't pay attention to the credit report or don't report inaccurate information.

How It Will Repair Your Credit

The basis is that section 609 gives you a legal loophole to create a letter requesting the credit bureau to erase the incorrect information that's showing up on your credit report. This is a letter they must reply to within 30 days. If they don't, you are then able to contact them again and tell them they have violated the law, and now they need to take the wrong charges off your credit report.

Once the erroneous information is removed from your credit report, your score will go up, and agencies will no longer be able to see this information.

CHAPTER 1:

Section 609 of the F.C.R.A

The Fair Credit Reporting Act is a Federal law in the U.S. that states that all three credit bureaus must verify any information that they receive from creditors and collection agencies before they add it into your credit report. Credit reporting agencies (CRA's) are required by law to obtain a copy of the original signed document from the time that you opened your loan. Since most accounts are reported to the bureaus digitally, it is hard for CRA's to accurately verify all accounts because there is no paperwork signed by you to prove that the statement was even yours to begin with.

Most people are not aware of Section 609in FCRA, so they do not know their rights. CRA's know that the public is not aware of their rights. If you were to simply write them a letter asking them to "verify" each account on your report, they would send you a message saying it's been verified or "yes," but they will not provide you with the proof. It is your LEGAL RIGHT to be provided with physical evidence that the account on your credit is yours. CRA's that do not comply with

Section 609 violates the FCRA! Whether the account is valid or not does matter.

The Fair Credit Reporting Act Section 609

Before we begin, you should NEVER dispute any of your credit reports online. When you do this, and they tell you that the account has been "verified," you are forfeiting your right to re-dispute that account. You always want to keep a paper-trail when dealing with these entities. It would be best for you to keep three separate files for every three bureaus so that it is easier to keep track of the letters you sent out and your progress.

It is recommended that you only dispute 22 accounts at a time. If you attempt to discuss more than this, the CRA's will classify your dispute as frivolous, and your claims may be overlooked. Be sure to include a copy of your social security card and a current driver's license/state-issued photo I.D. if you even want the CRA's to pay any attention to your letter. It is best to have them notarized as well, as this will be legal proof that it is you who have signed off on these letters.

It is a MUST that you send all letters with a tracking number; the best options are by certified mail or priority mail via USPS. Keep receipts for each message that you have mailed out for your files.

What Is Section 609 of the FCRA?

The Fair Credit Reporting Act (FCRA) includes many parts of credit checking to keep accuracy and privacy. It provides the duties of credit bureaus and credit reporting entities and companies together with the rights of the client – your rights.

For instance, under this act, you should be informed if any of the information from your file has been used against you. Additionally, you have the right to dispute information that may be incomplete or inaccurate. Other problems addressed include restricting third-party access to your file, asking your consent before giving your credit scores to workers, and the choice to look damage from those who violate the FCRA.

The FCRA is split up into sections, each with a different set of regulations for credit bureaus to observe. Section 609 of the FCRA deals with disclosure and place the burden of issuing proper documentation on the credit bureaus. In other words, you may have debt or negative items on your credit report, but there may be a way around them.

What does area 609 of the FCRA indeed state?

Numerous specifications that the FCRA presents are made to battle identity theft, and Section 609 is one of them. The reason for Section 609 is to make it increasingly hard for individuals to acquire credit data about others.

FCRA Section 609: Disclosure to client expresses that each customer has the option to demand divulgence of any data in their record, the wellsprings of the data, and the distinguishing proof of any individual who got your credit report.

What is more, if any credit report office neglects to check any of this data, they should expel the negative imprint from your credit report (which could, thus, improve your credit score).

Leasers need to keep incredibly precise and careful records of any of their exchanges with purchasers to report adverse action lawfully.

What Do I Need to Include in My Dispute?

The next thing that we are going to look at here is what we need to include in our 609 Letter. The more details that we can add in this, the better it is going to be for us overall. We do not want to prolong the process because the credit bureau is not sure what we are talking about, and we don't want to raise any red flags at all. When we send out some of these letters, we want to make sure that the dispute has the right information in place to help us see results.

When we are writing out some of the dispute letters here, it is essential that we go through and include all of the information that is relevant to our needs, along with a few other key elements, so that we can get a letter that is impactful and effective all rolled into one. A strong message is not only going to help make one of the best cases for you; it is going to make sure that you can hit on some of the points that you would like to emphasize and will tie all of this information back to the specific parts of Section 609 that you would like to highlight at this time.

Then it is time to bring in some of the relevant documentation. For each of the credit bureau's you would like to contact, you need to make sure that you are providing proof of your own identity along with the letter. The good news is that there are a few different options you can choose to help prove this one, including any documents that can verify your full name, your date of birth, and your social security number. Some of the options include:

1. A copy of your driver's license

2. Social security cards

3. Passport

4. Marriage certificate

5. Birth certificate

One of your W2 forms if it has your social security number on it.

You need to make sure that the verification that you want to use here is going to have your full name and your SSN on it. You also need to have some documents that are going to verify what your most current mailing address is. This could be found on the house deed, the mortgage, utility bills, rental agreement, driver's license, and more.

And of course, we need to make sure that we go through and have a copy of our credit score. You are not going to get very far if you do not have this credit report ready to go. You also need to go through and have all the relevant items highlighted on it to keep it already and organized.

We must make sure that we are working with the right references, statements, and wording to make this work. A mention of Section 609 that we are dealing with here and the exact portion that you would like to reference in your letter will be necessary. Each piece that you want to mention is going to be denoted with some combination of an uppercase, and a lowercase letter, a number, or Roman numeral based on what it is all about.

Send a Letter to Each Credit Agency

This document is a great way to challenge other and third-party collection agencies. The more the debt has been sold to other debt purchasers, the less likely that they have the legal proof and documents to prove that the debt is valid or that they can even collect on it. ONLY send this document to the collection agency in question, never to the credit bureau. Doing so may result in them going to the original creditor and update your credit file lowering your score. Make sure you notarize the document and send it via certified mail. Keep all copies as legal action may be needed.

One thing that we need to remember here is that we have to go through the process of sending out one of these Section 609 letters to each credit agency that we want to get to remove the items. The credit agencies are not going to talk to one another about this. If you send out a letter to Transunion, but not to one of the others, then Transunion may take it off your report, but none of the others would do this for you.

You must be responsible for sending a letter to all three of the reporting agencies if you would like to get that debt taken out of all your reports. You should automatically send this information to all three right from the start, so make sure to get copies of all the data so that you are ready to go and handle all of that at once as well.

You can include the same information in each of the letters that you send out. And you can even send out the same message, just make sure to change the company and department name that you are using on each one. Then include the identity proofs of your identity, the credit reports, and more, for each one to get the ball rolling here.

CHAPTER 2:

The Necessary Documents before
Sending the Letter

C redit bureaus held privately, billion-dollar organizations whose primary reason for existing is to make cash; that is what revenue driven organizations do, right? They keep data that lenders furnish them - regardless of whether accurate or inaccurate - about our credit association with them and sell it. Basic right? This straightforward plan of action generates over $4 Billion per year!

One wellspring of income for them originates from selling the information on our credit reports to different lenders, managers, insurance agencies, credit card organizations, and those you approve of to see your credit information. In addition to the fact that they provide raw data, they likewise sell them various methods for examining the data to decide the risk of stretching out credit to us. In addition to trading our information to lenders, they likewise sell our data to us. Credit scores, credit observing administrations, extortion security, and wholesale fraud prevention - interestingly enough, this region has quickly gotten perhaps the most significant wellspring of income. Furthermore, those pre-endorsed offers in our letter drop each week or garbage mail? That is right; they got our information from the credit bureaus as well. Organizations buy into assistance provided by the three credit bureaus that sell a rundown of consumer's credit information that fit pre-decided criteria.

Presently, as opposed to prevalent thinking, credit bureaus do not have any contribution. However, by utilizing the entirety of the set information on your credit report (personal information, payment history, and credit propensities) and FICO's technique for scoring that data, they tell them how creditworthy you are.

Origin and History of Credit Bureau

In recent decades credit has gotten more comfortable and easier to obtain. Credit cards, for example, were once given basically to the wealthier classes in the public eye and were utilized just occasionally. Toward the start of the twenty-first century, practically 50% of all Americans had in any event one broadly useful credit card (that is, a Visa, MasterCard, American Express, or Discover card). The ascent of credit as a typical method to buy necessities, extravagances, and everything in the middle of implies that credit bureaus process more information and are a more crucial part of the general economy than any other time in recent memory. Likewise, credit bureaus monitor and investigate the data obtained from a regularly expanding number of loans for homes, cars, and other high-cost things.

Today, credit bureaus consistently accumulate information from creditors. Banks; credit-card guarantors; mortgage organizations, which have practical experience in loaning cash to home buyers; and different businesses that stretch out credit to people and companies) and amass it into files on singular firms and consumers while refreshing their current records. In addition to the data gathered from creditors, credit files may likewise contain one's business history, previous addresses, false names, bankruptcy filings, and removals. Information usually remains on a credit report for seven years before being evacuated.

The more significant part of the nearby and provincial consumer credit bureaus in the United States is claimed by or are under agreement to one of the three essential consumer credit-reporting administrations referenced previously. Every one of these three organizations, assembles and appropriates information separately. Credit scores and reports vary somewhat from bureau to bureau. Each organization keeps up around 200 million single consumer credit files. Frequently a lender will utilize an average of the credit evaluations provided by the three different bureaus when choosing whether to make a loan.

The primary business credit bureau of the U.S. is Dun and Bradstreet. D and B have credit files on over 23 million associations in North America and more than 100 million businesses worldwide. In addition to giving creditors information essential to decide a credit applicant's capabilities, credit bureaus make their data accessible for progressively questionable purposes. For example, standard mail advertisers regularly buy information from credit bureaus as they continued looking for potential clients. If that you have ever gotten a letter revealing to you that you have been pre-endorsed for a credit card at a special yearly percentage rate, it is valid. The credit-card organization realizes your credit rating and must be sure previously affirmed you for the predefined card. Forthcoming managers and proprietors sometimes buy credit histories, as well.

CHAPTER 3:

Where to Send Your 609 Letters?

C redit bureaus collect information from various sources following consumer information. The activity is done for multiple reasons and includes data from singular consumers. Included is the information concerning a people charge payments and their getting. Utilized for evaluating creditworthiness, the info provides lenders with an outline of your accounts if a loan repayment is required. The interest rates charged on loan are additionally worked out concerning the kind of credit score shown by your experience. It is like this, not a uniform procedure, and your credit report is a vital instrument that affects future loans.

Based on risk-based valuing, it pegs various risks on the multiple customers in this manner, deciding the cost you will acquire as a borrower. Done as a credit rating, it is assistance provided to various interested parties in the public. Terrible credit histories are affected for the most part by settled court commitments, which mark you for high-interest rates every year. Duty liens and bankruptcies, for example, shut you out of the conventional credit lines and may require a great deal of arrangement for any loan to be offered by the bank.

Bureaus collect and examine credit information, including financial data, personal information, and elective data. Various sources give this generally marked data furnishers. These have an exceptional association with the credit bureaus. An average gathering of data furnishers would comprise of creditors, lenders, utilities, and debt collection agencies. Pretty much any association which has had payment involvement in the consumer is qualified, including courts. Any data collected for this situation is provided to the credit bureaus for grouping. When it is accumulated, the data is placed into specific repositories and files claimed by the bureau. The information is made accessible to customers upon request. The idea of such information is necessary for lenders and managers.

The information is in this manner material in various conditions; credit evaluation and business thought are simply part of these. The consumer may likewise require the data to check their score, and the home proprietor may need to check their inhabitant's report before renting an apartment. Since borrowers saturate the market, the ratings will, in general, be robotic. A straightforward examination would deal with this by giving the client a calculation for rapid appraisal, and checking your score once every other year should deal with errors in your report.

Individuals from the public are qualified for one free credit report from every one of the significant bureaus. Business reports, for example, Payed, might be gotten to on request and are chargeable. Lawful expressions for the credit bureaus incorporate credit report agency, CRA in the U.S. This is organized in the Fair Credit Report Act, FCTA. Other government rules associated with the assurance of the consumer incorporate Fair and Accurate Credit Transaction Act, Fair Credit Billing Act, and Regulation B. Statutory bodies have additionally been made for the regulation of the credit bureaus. The Fair-Trade Commission serves as a controller for the consumer credit report agencies. At the same time, the Office of the Comptroller of Currency fills in as a manager of all banks going about as furnishers.

CHAPTER 4:

The Three Main Credit Bureaus

The ideal approach to manage your credit capably and assume responsibility for your financial circumstance is to be educated. This takes a brief period and exertion on your part. Yet, since your credit scores are so crucial to dealing with your accounts and setting aside cash, you must know as much as you can regarding the credit bureaus that formulate credit appraisals. To assist you with getting a running beginning on that strategy's, some details on TransUnion, Experian and Equifax, the primary credit bureaus of the U.S.:

TransUnion

TransUnion has workplaces the nation over that manage various parts of credit: identity theft, credit management, and other credit issues; and types of credit customers, for example, personal, business, and press inquiries. If that you discover errors on your TransUnion credit report, you can call them at 800.916.8800 or visit their site to debate them. If that you believe that you are a casualty of identity theft, call them at 800.680.7289 at the earliest opportunity.

Experian

Like other credit bureaus, Experian provides a wide range of various administrations for people, businesses, and the media. Experian is based in Costa Mesa, CA, and has a website. Yet, if you discover errors in your report or need to report potential identity theft, this credit bureau makes it elusive telephone numbers on the site. Instead, they encourage guests to utilize online forms for questions, identity theft reports, and different issues.

Equifax

Based in Atlanta, GA, Equifax likewise has various departments to help people with multiple types of questions and concerns. Their website is additionally set up to have people utilize online forms to work on errors, report identity theft, and handle different matters. In any case, if somebody believes that their identity has been taken, the individual in question can, however, call 888.397.3742 to report it to Equifax. If that somebody detects a blunder on their Equifax credit report, that person must utilize the contact number on the story to question it. There is no number on the site to describe errors.

These are the three credit bureaus in the nation, and they each adopt an alternate strategy to enabling people to get in touch with them to pose inquiries or address any issues they might be encountering. Rather than reaching the credit bureaus legitimately, numerous people prefer to utilize a credit checking administration to assist them with dealing with their credit and stay over their funds. The credit bureaus all have related projects; however, most people prefer to utilize an independent organization to assist them with these issues. That way, they get an impartial perspective on their credit score and a lot more devices to manage and improve their credit ratings proactively.

Dealing with Credit Bureaus

Today, where the economy is at its weak point, having good credit is a necessary tool. This is because it allows you to obtain house loans, car loans, credit cards, and other convenient financial services and instruments. You may be able to live without having good credit. You can discern the credit bureau that holds your file by looking at any rejection letter you received from a recent credit application. If you are dealing with the credit bureau that handles your data, keep in mind that it belongs in the business of collecting and selling information. As such, you should not provide them with any detail, which is not necessarily legally. When you already have your credit report, make sure to check for any error or discrepancy. If you find anything that is questionable in your story, you can send the credit bureau a written request for them to investigate the failure. In general, the credit bureau has the burden of documenting anything that is included in your credit report. If the credit bureau fails to investigate the error or neglects your request for an investigation within 30 days, the error should be removed. You need to educate yourself about the legal obligations of credit bureaus to have a successful credit repair process. Before dealing with them, make sure you know all the legal aspects so you would not end up paying for something that should not be charged with a fee. Remember, credit bureaus are also businesses and that they own many credit repairs companies.

Making the Best of Credit Bureaus

It is a little annoying to learn that all three credit bureaus have sensitive financial data. However, there is no method to prevent lenders and collection entities from sharing your information with the above companies. You can limit any possible problems associated with the credit bureaus by evaluating your credit reports annually and acting immediately in case you notice some errors. It is also good to monitor your credit cards and other open credit products to ensure that no one is misusing the accounts. If you have a card that you do not often use, sign up for alerts on that card so that you get notified if any transactions happen, and regularly review statements for your active tickets. Next, if you notice any signs of fraud or theft, you can choose to place a credit freeze with the three credit bureaus and be diligent in tracking the activity of your credit card in the future.

How the Bureaus Get Their Information

To learn how the score gets calculated, first, we need to learn about all the different inputs of your score, aka where the bureaus get their info. You may have many factors that report information to the credit bureaus or none. Credit cards are called revolving accounts or revolving debt by the credit bureaus. Each monthly payment and balance are reported, as well as any late payments. This means that any cards that have your name on them will also report to all the bureaus. This includes cards that belong to a spouse or parent. If you are an authorized user on the account, it gets reported on your credit no matter what. Many people have their credit ruined by a spouse or parent going into bankruptcy or not paying their credit card bills. If your name is on any credit card that belongs to people that may not pay their bills, ask them to take your name off immediately! Installment loans also report information to the credit bureaus. If you went down to your local Sears and financed a washer/dryer set by putting up a down payment, that is an installment loan. The details of these loans are all reported; the total balance, as well as the timeliness and amounts of your monthly payments. If you have mortgages or student loans, that information does get reported. Total amounts due, total paid so far, and the status of monthly payments is all reported. This information is kept track of and organized in their databases.

CHAPTER 5:

What A 609 Letter Can and Cannot Do

When the revealing credit office gets your Section 609 letter, it will either react by sending you the agreement with your mark on it that underpins the furnisher's guarantee or inform you that it doesn't have the first agreement.

The organization may erase the data from your document without you doing whatever else. Be that as it may, if the off-base data remains, you will need to make the following stride and dispute it with the revealing credit organization once more. On the contest structure, call attention to that you or the credit revealing office cannot confirm the data, so it should be expelled. This ought to work.

You can document online disputes with every one of the three credit departments through their sites.

Then again, if the credit report office can deliver the mentioned unique agreement with your mark, the data will stay set up until it drops off your credit report when it is coordinated out. Most negative data (for example, late installments, defaults, charge-offs, and obligations that were sent to gatherers) can remain on a credit report for a long time. A liquidation will stay for a long time from the recording date.

Know that Section 609 gives you the option to demand data about the things recorded on your credit reports, but not explicitly to dispute them. Such questions are canvassed in Sections 611 and 623 of the FCRA. Numerous customers have discovered that revealing credit organizations will evacuate strange data in the wake of accepting the Section 609 letter.

Do not sit around time composing and sending these letters if you realize the culpable credit report data is right. Regardless of the ruckus encompassing 609 messages, they do not escape obligation-free cards. They are to be utilized sincerely and sensibly. Whatever else is the maltreatment of the procedure?

What 609 letters do not do?

It is imperative to realize that while a 609 letter may help with your credit repair, they don't soothe you of your obligation. If it is an authentic obligation, you are yet liable for taking care of it.

Something else you ought to know about is that an expelled thing could be reinserted if the lender is later ready to check the data on your credit report being referred to.

Along these lines, even though the credit report agencies will erase a thing if a leaser does not react inside 30 days, they, despite everything, reserve the option to create their proof sometime in the future.

Furthermore, ultimately, if a bank has offered your record to an obligation assortment organization, you may see a similar obligation spring up again with the other organization.

This can occur with accounts you, despite everything, owe cash on if you keep on being reprobate. You effectively dispute a thing with your unique loan boss along these lines, and it may not be its finish.

If this occurs, you should experience the dispute procedure again with the assortment organizations to attempt to get those expelled also.

Recruit a Credit Repair Agency if You Need Help with a Dispute

As should be obvious, there are many strides to building up a 609 letter, and it is essential to be careful and exact. On the off chance that you are in a period crunch since you're in the market for a Visa or credit, or are baffled with the procedure and need assistance, don't stop for a second to go to the aces for help.

What is a 609-credit dispute letter?

You may have the option to get negative things expelled from your credit report depending on Section 609, and numerous others have had achievement, which boosts their credit score.

The essential procedure includes composing a letter to request a check of all the data in your record with the expectation that something was not archived accurately. On the off chance that the loan boss did neglect to file something effectively, they have no lawful decision yet to expel that negative thing from your credit report. This is the reason it is regularly called a credit repair "loophole" in the system. Common questions state a negative thought is off base or does not have a place with the individual. Yet, a 609 letter dispute says the situation may have a home with you, yet if they can't demonstrate that you consented to have somebody pull your credit report, they need to expel it—so this can fill in as a pleasant credit repair choice.

Hiring a Credit Repair Company

Some companies represent themselves as credit repair specialists as well as law firms that specialize in credit repair. While many of them are responsible, honest entities, some aren't. A reputable credit repair company won't promise a particular result. If you do decide to hire such a firm, you shouldn't have to pay them upfront. Generally, you'll save money and get the job done taking care of things by yourself, and using a credit repair firm is not recommended. Still, if your time is particularly valuable or your situation complicated, it might be worth it.

Negotiating

If you have a default on a credit card account, contact your creditor and ask them to remove it from your record (or mark it "Paid as agreed.") in return for your paying off the debt. Make sure they provide a written statement saying they agree to do this when you pay off the balance.

CHAPTER 6:

Hire a Credit Repair Agency If You Need Help With a Dispute

The FAIR CREDIT REPORTING ACT states that all credit agencies such as Equifax, Experian, and Transunion must verify every single transaction along with all information they receive from the credit card companies and banks alike, every single month BEFORE it can be placed onto your credit report.

This means that the CRA's must-have ORIGINAL SIGNED DOCUMENTS from when your credit card was opened and or when you acquired a loan. And herein lies your Quick-Smart-Credit 609 Solution to your current credit conundrum.

Think about this: Since hundreds of millions of accounts need wet signed paperwork to be considered as verified documentation every single month, month after month, and year after year, the regulatory costs are deemed to be too high to justify. Therefore, it is not a protocol action for officials to act - on. It certainly does not cost worthy enough for any government agency to verify all the recurring accounts repeatedly.

Government spending is continuously scrutinized by the people (you and I), which is a good thing. And since the uprising of this beautiful new digital age we live in, all possible recurring documentation that can be documented electronically must then be filed as such, with no paper.

In other words, no paper records for document verification exist for that reason alone. As well, the number of new bodies on payroll needed to do all this non-existent verifying would incur even more regulatory costs. And this is what would be officially considered as frivolous spending each month. Even if the people existed to do so. Thus, there are no government employees also to verify them. No verification system, no employee testing, means no verification is getting done. It is a simple math equation when it comes down to it.

The FCRA is a complicated law that bears looking into a little more deeply. Likewise, just because it protects you in a wide variety of ways doesn't mean the credit reporting agency or creditors are always going to follow it the way they should. What follows are several common ways the FCRA is violated regularly.

Reporting or furnishing old information: While credit bureaus and creditors are required to keep your details as up to date as possible, you will frequently find that they fail to do so in several keyways. They will often fail to report that a given debt was discharged because bankruptcy was filed, that an old debt is either re-engaged or completely new, indicate that a closed account is active when it has been closed or keep information that is more past than seven years (ten for bankruptcies) on your credit report. If you report these errors, they are legally required to look into them within 30 days.

Reporting blatantly inaccurate information: Creditors are not allowed to provide information to credit bureaus that they know, or should know, is inaccurate. It includes classifying debt as charged-off when it was paid in full, altering balances due, reporting a timely payment as late, listing you as the debtor when you were only an authorized user on a specific account and failing to mention when identity fraud was suspected or confirmed for a given account. Again, if you report these errors, they are legally required to look into them.

Mixing up files: While it may seem surprising, credit reporting agencies frequently mix up data on individuals, potentially harming your credit score for someone else's mistakes. These issues can arise between individuals who have similar social security numbers if you are a Junior or a Senior, and the problem is with the other person's credit, mixing up details when names are similar or even mixing up features for two people with the same zip code.

Violations of debt dispute with credit reporting agencies: Credit reporting agencies have to follow strict rules when it comes to handling disputes; nevertheless, there are frequently issues with the ways they follow through on the process. It includes failing to notify you that a dispute has been received, failing to investigate the dispute in a timely fashion, and failing to correct disputes on time.

Creditor debt dispute violations: The FCRA also has strict rules when it comes to how creditors must handle disputes, which are frequently disregarded. These violations include things like not notifying credit reporting agencies that a debt is being disputed, not submitting corrected information after the debt has been successfully disputed, not conducting internal investigations into the dispute once they have been notified of the error, making it challenging to submit disputes and not informing you of the results of the study into the dispute within five days after it has been completed.

Inaccurate credit report requests: Just because specific individuals are allowed to see your credit report doesn't mean they are allowed to do so at all times. The FCRA ensures that your credit report can't be accessed to determine if you are worth filing a lawsuit against, can't be accessed by employers without express permission, and can't be accessed by previous creditors related to debts that have been discharged for bankruptcy just to see what your current financial activity is.

What Are My Rights Under 609?

The Fair Credit Reporting Act is going to cover a lot of the aspects and the components of credit checking to make sure that it can maintain a reasonable amount of privacy and accuracy along the way. This agency is going to list all the responsibilities that credit reporting companies and any credit bureaus will have, and it also includes the rights of the consumer, which will be your rights in this situation. This act is going to be the part that will govern how everything is going to work to ensure that all parties are treated fairly.

When using this act, the consumer has to be told if any of the information that is on your file has been in the past or is now being used against you in any way, shape, or form. You have a right to know whether the information is harming you and what that information is.

Besides, the consumer is going to have the right to go through and dispute any information that may be inaccurate or incomplete at the time. If they see that there are items in the documents they are sent, if the billing to them is not right or there is something else off in the process, the consumer has the right to dispute this. The credit reporting agency needs to determine at least if the consumer is right.

This act is going to limit the access that third parties can have to your file. You must go through and provide your consent before someone can go through and look at your credit score, whether it is a potential employer or another institution providing you with funding.

They are not able to get in and just look at it. Keep in mind that if you do not agree for them to take a look at the information, it is going to likely result in you not getting the funding that you want, because there are very few ways that the institution can fairly assess the risk that you pose to them in terms of creditworthiness.

It means that you may have debt or another negative item that is on your credit report, but there is a way to get around this without having to wait for years to get that to drop off your story or having to pay back a debt that you are not able to afford.

Keep in mind that this is not meant to be a method for you to take on a lot of debts that you cannot afford and then just dump them. But on occasion, there could be a few that you can fight and get an instant boost to your credit score in the process.

CHAPTER 7:

Section 609 Is Designed To Protect You?

The 609 Letter is going to be one of the newest credit repair secrets that will help you to remove a lot of information on your credit report, all of the false information, and sometimes even the accurate information, thanks to a little loophole that is found in our credit reporting laws.

If you have spent a bit of time trying to see some increase in your credit score, you may find that the 609 letter is the right thing to do to get some of the negative accounts, the ones that are pulling your credit score down quite a bit, taken from your report. You can use this kind of letter to resolve some of the inaccuracies that show up, to dispute your errors, and handle some of the other items that could inaccurately come in and impact and lower your credit score.

When it is time to report your credit history at all, one of the credit bureau's is going to be responsible for including not only correct information but also the accuracy of the report. The use of this letter in credit repair is going to be based mostly on the idea of whether the credit bureau was responsible for how they verified the information they put onto the report, and if they can do it promptly.

Credit bureaus are going to collect information on consumer credit from a lot of different sources like banks. Then they are going to be able to resell that information to any business who would like to evaluate the credit applications of the clients. Credit bureaus are going to be governed by the FCRA or the Fair Credit Reporting Act, which is going to help detail what credit reporting agencies and information furnishers can and can't do when they decide to report information on the consumer.

Using these 609 letters is the right way for us to clean up our credit a bit, and in some cases, it is going to make a perfect situation. However, we must remember that outside of some of the obvious benefits that we are going to discuss, and there are a few things that we need to be aware of ahead of time.

Few limitations are going to come with this as well. For example, even after you work with the 609 letters, it is possible that the information will later be seen as accurate could be added to the report again, even after the removal. This is going to happen if the creditor, after the fact, can verify the accuracy. They may take it off for a bit if the 30 days have passed, and they are not able to confirm at that point. But if the information is accurate, remember that it could end up back on the report.

New debt collection agencies could go through and add some more outstanding debts to your credit report at any time. This could bring the score back down, especially if you are not careful about the way that you spend your money and handle debts along the way.

While some people think that it is possible, keep in mind that you are not able to eliminate any obligations to repay a legitimate debt. Even if you write out a 609 letter and you can get that debt removed from the credit report, whether that is for the short term or a longer-term, you still have to pay that legitimate debt. Do not use this to hide from your debts or get from paying them at all. Use this as a method that will help you to clear out some of the older options, or some of the debts that you have taken care of but remain on your reports.

Besides, contrary to some of the myths that are out there when it comes to these 609 letters, the FCRA is not going to require that any of the credit agencies keep or provide signed contracts or proof of debts. You can, however, ask them to give you description of the procedure that they used to complete the investigation into your accounts. The FCRA, though, is going to give you as a consumer the right to go through and dispute some of the errors that show up on your credit report. This is not a way for you to go through and make some of your student loans or other debts go away, so you do not have to pay them any longer. But it is going to be one of the best ways that you can get information that is not accurately taken off the credit report. We can get a lot of things done when we work with the Section 609 letters, but they are not a magic pill that will make things disappear for us. They will make it easier for us to go through and get rid of information that is not correct and can ensure that we can get rid of debts that maybe we settled in the past but are still harming our credit. This is going to make it easier overall for us to ensure that we can get things organized and get a higher credit score that we are looking for.

How to File a Dispute with Section 609

It is important to note that there are several template letters for section 609. What this means is that you can easily download and use one of these templates yourself. While you usually have to pay for them, there are some which are free. Of course, you will want to remember to include your information in the letter before you send it.

However, many people suggest that you do not use one of the online templates. While they have worked in some cases, it is always best to do the work you need to do to make sure you get the best results. Think of it this way - you are creating a letter to try to remove the wrong information from your credit report. You will want to make sure everything is done correctly, as this will make it more likely that the information will come off, and no one will place it back on your report again.

However, if you do decide to use the template as a guide, which is completely fine if you have all the information you need, below are the steps to complete this.

1. Find a dispute letter through googling "section 609 dispute letter". While you might be able to find a free download, for some, you will be able to copy and paste into Microsoft Word or onto a Google Doc.

2. Make the necessary changes to the letter. This will include changing the name and address. You will also want to make sure your phone number is included. Sometimes people include their email address, but this is not necessary. It is always safer to only include your home address or P.O.box information. You will also want to make sure to edit the whole letter. If something does not match up to what you

want to say in your message, such as what you are trying to dispute on your credit report, you need to state this. These letters are quite generic, which means you need to add in your information.

3. You want to make sure that all your account information you want to be taken off your credit report is handwritten. You also want to make sure you use blue ink rather than black. On top of this, you do not need to worry about being too neat, but you want to make sure they can read the letters and numbers correctly. This is an integral part of filing your dispute letter because handwritten ones in blue ink will not be pushed through their automated system. They have an automatic system that will read the letter for them and punch in the account number you use. They will then send you a generic message that states these accounts are now off your credit report, which does not mean that it happened. When you write the information down, a person needs to read it and will typically take care of it. Of course, this does not mean that you will not be pushed aside. Unfortunately, this can happen with any letters.

4. You want to make sure that you prove who you are with your letters. While this is never an easy thing to do, you must send a copy of your social security card and your driver's license, or they will shred your letter. You also need to make sure that you get each of your messages notarized. You can typically do this by visiting your county's courthouse.

5. You can send as many letters as you need to; however, keep in mind that the creditor typically will not make you submit more than four. This is because when you threaten to take them to court in the third

letter, they will realize that your accounts and demands just are not worth it. First, you could damage their reputation, and secondly, you will cost them more money than only taking the information off your credit report will.

6. You will want to make sure that you keep all correspondence they send you. This will come in handy when they try to make you send more information or keep telling you that they cannot do anything. You must not give up. Many people struggle to get them to pay attention because that is just how the system works. Therefore, you need to make sure that you do not listen to their quick automatic reply that your information is of your credit report. You also want to make sure to wait at least three months and then re-run your credit report to make sure the wrong information has been removed. Keep track of every time you need to re-run your credit report as you can use this as proof if they continue to send you a letter stating the information is off of your credit report. It is important to note that you can now file a dispute letter online with all three credit bureaus. However, this is a new system, which means that it does come with more problems than sending one through the mail. While it is ultimately your choice whether you use a form to file your 609 dispute or send a letter, you always want to make sure you keep copies and continue to track them, even if you don't hear from the credit bureau after a couple of months. It will never hurt to send them a second letter or even a third.

CHAPTER 8:

What In Section 609, You Have the Right to Request

How these works are by first disputing a thing with the credit report authorities legitimately. Each credit authority has a connection to discuss any of your credit things so you can do this on the web if you wish, or you can submit one recorded as a hard copy by sending them a letter.

Now and then, a credit report office will evacuate a thing after your first question, yet frequently, you will be required to catch up with further documentation.

For instance, if a thing contains an equalization mistake, you may need to send receipts or other verification that shows why you trust it is off base.

The credit departments' duty

A significant part of the duty regarding exact announcing falls on the credit report authorities.

That is the reason, and often, the question procedure begins with them.

As indicated by the FCRA, credit report organizations are required to remember just exact and unquestionable data for your credit report.

This implies is that if the credit agency does not get palatable reactions from your loan bosses, they are committed to expelling any negative things from your credit report.

How to File a Dispute with Section 609

It is important to note that there are several template letters for section 609. What this means is that you can easily download and use one of these templates yourself. While you usually must pay for them, there are some which are free. Of course, you will want to remember to include your information in the letter before you send it.

However, many people suggest that you do not use one of the online templates. While they have worked in some cases, it is always best to do the work you need to do to make sure you get the best results. Think of it this way - you are creating a letter to try to remove the wrong information from your credit report. You will want to make sure everything is done correctly, as this will make it more likely that the information will come off, and no one will place it back on your report again. However, if you do decide to use the template as a guide, which is completely fine if you have all the information you need, below are the steps to complete this.

1. Find a dispute letter through googling "section 609 dispute letter". While you might be able to find a free download, for some, you will be able to copy and paste into Microsoft Word or onto a Google Doc.

47

2. Make the necessary changes to the letter. This will include changing the name and address. You will also want to make sure your phone number is included. Sometimes people include their email address, but this is not necessary. It is always safer to only include your home address or P.O.box information. You will also want to make sure to edit the whole letter. If something does not match up to what you want to say in your message, such as what you are trying to dispute on your credit report, you need to state this. These letters are quite generic, which means you need to add in your information.

3. You want to make sure that all your account information you want to be taken off your credit report is handwritten. You also want to make sure you use blue ink rather than black. On top of this, you don't need to worry about being too neat, but you want to make sure they can read the letters and numbers correctly. This is an essential part of filing your dispute letter because handwritten ones in blue ink will not be pushed through their automated system. They have an automatic mode that will read the letter for them and punch in the account number you use. They will then send you a generic message that states these accounts are now off your credit report, which does not mean that it happened. When you write the information down, a person needs to read it and will typically take care of it. Of course, this does not mean that you will not be pushed aside. Unfortunately, this can happen with any letters.

4. You want to make sure that you prove who you are with your letters. While this is never an easy thing to do, you must send a copy of

your social security card and your driver's license, or they will shred your letter. You also need to make sure that you get each of your messages notarized. You can typically do this by visiting your county's courthouse.

5. You can send as many letters as you need to; however, keep in mind that the creditor typically will not make you submit more than four. This is because when you threaten to take them to court in the third letter, they will realize that your accounts and demands just are not worth it. First, you could damage their reputation, and secondly, you will cost them more money than only taking the information off your credit report will.

6. You will want to make sure that you keep all correspondence they send you. This will come in handy when they try to make you send more information or keep telling you that they cannot do anything. You must not give up. Many people struggle to get them to pay attention because that is just how the system works. Therefore, you need to make sure that you do not listen to their quick automatic reply that your information is of your credit report. You also want to make sure to wait at least three months and then re-run your credit report to make sure the wrong information has been removed. Keep track of every time you need to re-run your credit report as you can use this as proof if they continue to send you a letter stating the information is of your credit report.

CHAPTER 9:

Contrary To What Some Might Think, Section 609 Does Not

I f you notice anything on your report that should not be there, you need to use the section 609 loophole to file a dispute, which could result in their wrong information being taken off of the report. If this is the case, your credit score will increase as you will no longer have this harmful inaccuracy affecting your score.

How to File a Dispute with Section 609

It is important to note that there are several template letters for section 609. What this means is that you can easily download and use one of these templates yourself. While you usually must pay for them, there are some which are free. Of course, you will want to remember to include your information in the letter before you send it.

You will want to make sure everything is done correctly, as this will make it more likely that the information will come off, and no one will place it back on your report again.

1. Find a dispute letter through googling "section 609 dispute letter". While you might be able to find a free download, for some, you will be able to copy and paste into Microsoft Word or onto a Google Doc.

2. Make the necessary changes to the letter. This will include changing the name and address. You will also want to make sure your phone number is included. Sometimes people include their email address, but this is not necessary. It is always safer to only include your home address or P.O.box information. You will also want to make sure to edit the whole letter. If something does not match up to what you want to say in your message, such as what you are trying to dispute on your credit report, you need to state this. These letters are quite generic, which means you need to add in your information.

3. You want to make sure that all your account information you want to be taken off your credit report is handwritten. You also want to make sure you use blue ink rather than black. On top of this, you do not need to worry about being too neat, but you want to make sure they can read the letters and numbers correctly. This is an essential part of filing your dispute letter because handwritten ones in blue ink will not be pushed through their automated system. They have an automatic mode that will read the letter for them and punch in the account number you use. They will then send you a generic message that states these accounts are now off your credit report, which does not mean that it happened. When you write the information down, a person needs to read it and will typically take care of it. Of course, this does not mean that you will not be pushed aside. Unfortunately, this can happen with any letters.

4. You want to make sure that you prove who you are with your letters. While this is never an easy thing to do, you must send a copy of

your social security card and your driver's license, or they will shred your letter. You also need to make sure that you get each of your messages notarized. You can typically do this by visiting your county's courthouse.

5. You can send as many letters as you need to; however, keep in mind that the creditor typically will not make you submit more than four. This is because when you threaten to take them to court in the third letter, they will realize that your accounts and demands just are not worth it. First, you could damage their reputation, and secondly, you will cost them more money than only taking the information off your credit report will.

6. You will want to make sure that you keep all correspondence they send you. This will come in handy when they try to make you send more information or keep telling you that they cannot do anything. You must not give up. Many people struggle to get them to pay attention because that is just how the system works. Therefore, you need to make sure that you do not listen to their quick automatic reply that your information is of your credit report. You also want to make sure to wait at least three months and then re-run your credit report to make sure the wrong information has been removed. Keep track of every time you need to re-run your credit report as you can use this as proof if they continue to send you a letter stating the information is off of your credit report.

It is important to note that you can now file a dispute letter online with all three credit bureaus. However, this is a new system, which means that it does come with more problems than sending one through the mail. While it is ultimately your choice whether you use a form to file your 609 dispute or send a letter, you always want to make sure you keep copies and continue to track them, even if you don't hear from the credit bureau after a couple of months. It will never hurt to send them a second letter or even a third.

CHAPTER 10:

How Does a 609 Letter Work

Now that you've reviewed your credit reports, credit scores, and credit history, you're ready to start thinking about what you can do to start pushing it upwards. Take each category of the FICO credit score, look at your history, and ask how you can improve that category.

You should begin by grouping problems you identified from your credit report review in a way that makes the most sense to you.

Consider creating a separate email account for your credit rating efforts. It will make it easier to keep related emails organized.

Here's one approach to organizing your tasks:

Quick and easy: if you have some credit inquiries that will expire soon, there's nothing you need to do, except be careful about applying for new credit. Using some of your savings to reduce your debt load on a credit card that's near its limit is pretty simple, so long as you have the money to do so.

Moderate effort: if you found any discrepancies in any of your credit reports, you should contact the appropriate credit reporting company to see if you can get the error corrected. Remember, both the credit reporting companies and creditors, "… are responsible for correcting inaccurate or incomplete information in your credit report," according to the FTC. Each of the three companies concerned has web pages specifically for customer disputes.

More effort: you can probably get a creditor to remove a late payment from your account record (more on this in a few lines). Another strategy you can consider is to take out a debt consolidation loan (more on this in a few lines too). It's a riskier strategy, so it needs to be carefully considered.

If you've found a discrepancy in your credit report, writing a letter to the responsible credit reporting company should be one of the first things you do. The FTC even provides you with a sample letter at its web site

The FTC recommends you send the letter via certified mail "return receipt requested." It also says to include copies (not originals) of any relevant documents or receipts you have. It can also help to send a copy of the page from your credit report with the item(s) circled.

While you can probably get things done via company web sites, going the paper route gives you a physically documented record of your efforts. While you hopefully won't need it, hard evidence can be easier to work with and be more reliable than electronic records.

Get Your Stuff Together

It helps to be organized. Create a binder or file and start gathering any records that will help you make your case with the various companies you're going to need to communicate. Make sure you have either web sites or email addresses for your creditors. Small businesses might not offer much when it comes to web sites, but you can count on the major credit card companies to have functional web sites that include ways you can contact them for help or disputes. They usually have live support available online too. Remember, if you're communicating in real-time, be prepared ahead of time and have at least an outline of what you want to cover in your call. It is one advantage of using the mail to make your dispute, and you're much more likely to submit all the necessary proof. Make sure you have the original of everything you sent in your dispute.

Your Checklist

Put together a checklist with deadlines to help keep you on track. Organize by the approach you like best. You can go from easy to hard, get going on the stuff that will take longer to get a response on, then knock off the faster stuff, so while the slow-moving chores and winding their way through the mail or a company bureaucracy, you can be getting things done.

Removing late payment codes: try to get as many of these removed as you can. Late payments take seven years to clear from your credit history, so trying to get as many as you can be removed can be a big help.

You are correcting errors: misspellings, incorrect information, and erroneous accounts. Credit bureaus have 30 days to investigate your complaint. You can use the mail system or web site for Equifax or

TransUnion. Experian only accepts requests online. You can find phone numbers, web addresses, and mail addresses for each company (if offered) *here*. One thing to look at extra strictly is anything listed by collections agencies. Consumer debt has a legal expiration date. Once that date has passed, you can't be forced to pay it. Collection agencies can still make an effort to collect that debt and will even sell the debt to other collectors who then try their luck collecting the debt. In the process, the dates recorded for that debt can be misreported, requiring correction. Of course, if a debt collector contacted you and you agreed to pay anything back (whether you paid any money or not), the clock on the debt begins from that point on.

Reducing debt ratios on credit cards: try to avoid having any tickets that are near their limits if you can. Considering transferring a balance if you can do so without doing anything to make your report worse (such as applying for a new card to shift the balance to). Paying down the cards is ideal if you have the money.

Disputing items: this is a little different than correcting errors. Here you're trying to get things off your report that maybe are justified. Still, if you can convince the creditor to remove the item, it's to your advantage, and let's face it, it's not like you're going to bully a big credit card company into doing something it doesn't want to do. Even disputing an old negative charge can sometimes pay off simply because the creditor may not respond.

Clearing civil judgments: these also appear on your credit history, so if you can pay them off or get them discharged, it will benefit your credit score.

CHAPTER 11:

Does A 609 Letter Really Improve My Credit?

While one's economic situation is different from another person, most people may be in some debt at a particular time. For instance, you may have small debts such as in-store financing or credit card bills, while others may have large ones such as mortgages and loans. This translates that almost everyone is most likely dependent on having a specific amount of credit. This is because confidence can be useful for some things.

As mentioned earlier, your credit report, which is held by a credit bureau, is significant to your credit status. The credit bureau will send you a notification when you are in default or missed payments to your creditors. Once you receive such notices, expect that you are in for a poor credit rating.

There are various steps involved in effective credit repair. These steps are particular to the situation of an individual. One of the most common actions that people in a bad credit situation take is debt consolidation.

If you are attempting to have your credit repaired, it is a principal act as quickly as possible. Once you miss out on payments to your creditors, your credit rating will be damaged almost immediately.

However, if you continuously miss your payments, the more damaged your credit rating will be.

You might be one of the numerous people who get confused that credit is simply "good" or "bad," and once you are in trouble with a creditor, it is a futile effort to repair it. On the contrary, even if you are in a bad credit situation, credit repair enables you to pay off your debts the quickest way possible. However, most people avoid any credit repair strategies because first off, they do not have money to pay their debts. For instance, you may have an unfortunate economic situation, which is why you missed out on your payments. This is the reason why a debt consolidation is an efficient tool, which can help you in repairing your credit.

Debt consolidation, as the name implies, consolidates all of your debts into just one loan. This means that if you have outstanding debts from various creditors, you can secure a loan from just one company and use the loan amount to pay your outstanding debts. You will only make your payments on a single loan and a single creditor/company.

Through debt consolidation, you will be able to have flexibility when your debts are already unmanageable. While you would still owe the same amount of money, debt consolidation allows you to secure a loan over the long term to lower your monthly payments. Furthermore, debt consolidation will enable you to improve your relationship with your creditors and paves the way for repairing your credit. Through debt consolidation, your creditors will report to credit bureaus that your debts are already cleared up; thus, the credit repair process can start quickly.

Ultimately, debt consolidation changes your status with your creditors in a quick manner. It stops the damage to your financial situation before it gets worse. You can be on good terms with just a single creditor as compared to being on bad terms with multiple ones. Besides, debt consolidation allows you to breathe before engaging in credit repair.

CHAPTER 12:

Correctly Disputing Errors on Your Credit Report

Time and again, it is mentioned that credit ratings are based on credit reports. Once your loan from a bank, credit card companies, or other financial institutions, they report your status to a credit bureau, including your terms of payment, your timeliness in making your payments, etc. In turn, the credit bureau records any information provided to them into a credit report, which serves as the key to your credit rating.

Unfortunately, once you obtain negative markets on your credit rating, it will remain in your credit report for seven years. This will prevent you from securing most types of loans. Your creditor will carry out different steps to make you pay your debt once you miss out on payments, regardless if it is a loan, financing, or credit card debt. More often than not, creditors give notices or warnings for an extended period. Eventually, though, they will sell your debt to a collection's agency. In this case, your creditors write-off the loan efficiently, given that they are selling your mortgage at a considerable discount.

Once your creditors decide that they have small chances of recovering the loan from you, they will take the loss by selling your debt to a collection's agency even by half of the loan amount. As they do this, you will be reported to the credit bureau, leaving you with the lowest possible mark that will affect your credit rating for seven years.

One significant step to repairing your credit is to avoid making your creditor's write-off your debt. When you are contacted by a collection's agent, make sure you act as soon as possible. First, you should contact your creditor and see if you can make arrangements to clear your debt with them. More often than not, when you agree to pay the debt at once, the creditor will remove the mark, "gone to collection" from your credit rating, which is necessary for a quick credit repair. However, if your creditor does not agree with this arrangement, you have no choice but to stick with the collection's agency.

At this point, your debt is already handed to a collection's agency and that the negative mark on your credit report cannot get any worse than it already is. As such, you need to take into consideration your options for credit repair.

In general, the collections agent will demand aggressively that you pay the debt immediately and in full. He/she will also imply that you will be taken to court if you refuse to pay at once. When this happens, keep in mind that the collections agency has already bought your debt at, more or less, half its value. Thus, when you pay higher than that, the collections agency will profit.

If your circumstances would allow, you can offer the collections agency an arrangement that you will pay immediately less than half of your debt's full value. In many cases, the collections agent will try to close your file to avoid extending the process. Such an arrangement is usually accepted by most collections' agencies.

If you want to repair your credit as soon as possible, it is best to pay your creditor instead of the collection's agency. However, if your financial status would not allow you to do so, make an offer to the agency to lower the figure rather than paying the full loan amount. Keep in mind that paying a collections agency in total should be your last resort.

CHAPTER 13:

Should You Pay For A 609 Credit Repair Letter?

I t would take a great deal of skill to master the area of budgeting. Some people may be better than others when it comes to managing their finances as well as maintaining good credit standing. If you have any type of debt from a creditor or financial institution, it is best to learn how to manage your debt properly. This way, apart from keeping a good credit standing, you will also be allowed to secure credit when you need one in the future. On the other hand, if you miss out on payments towards your debts or will enable them to go in default, you will be stuck with a negative mark, robbing you of economic opportunities.

If you want to repair your credit, it is essential to build up your credit rating again. One way of doing this is to consult or seek help from a credit counselor. Often, non-profit agencies carry out credit counseling. Some people confuse them with for-profit credit repair agencies, which often have a negative reputation due to scams, specifically those companies that advertise online. Other for-profit companies that are not scams are likely inclined to doing nothing that you cannot do on your own. For instance, they will simply instruct you to get a copy of your credit report and challenge any mistake on it. Some may even lead you to do illegal activities such as obtaining a "new" credit rating by using a different address.

One of the most common problems with credit repair companies, which you should be aware of is they tend to propose a quick, and one size fits all solution to any type of credit situation.

Thus, if you encounter someone who claims he/she can fix your credit quickly without knowing about your credit situation is not being truthful.

On the contrary, credit counseling services are there to provide you with advice regarding your attempt for credit repair.

Consulting a credit counselor is said to be the best way to do for people who want to repair their credit. This is because credit counselors can provide long term decisions and plans for efficient credit repair. They can also provide you with workshops and educational materials that help in understanding your credit as well as repairing it.

Most credit counseling companies help people to learn, creating, and to stick to a budget, which can be beneficial for credit rating over the long term. Besides, these companies usually carry out one-on-one counseling for their clients so that they can learn and analyze one's credit situation. Consequently, they can provide the best economic decisions based on specific credit status.

Credit counselors are crucial in providing a specific kind of attention, which most credit repair companies tend to avoid. If you decide to seek the help of credit counselors for repairing your credit, the solutions will usually be for the long term, given that you will be taught how to manage and control your budget efficiently.

Furthermore, you will also learn how to deal with permanent changes when it comes to your spending habits. By far, using a credit counseling company is most preferred when it comes to repairing credit.

CHAPTER 14:

How Long Does a 609 Credit Repair Take

I t is time to address a potential area of contention for some. Maybe you are just now starting to look into what your credit score is like, and to your horror, your credit score is not what you thought it was. Or perhaps instead, you've run into some harder times recently, and your credit has taken a hit of which you're aware.

How Long Will It Take to Repair Your Bad Credit?

Knowing how long it will take to repair your bad credit can help to not only provide you with more knowledge but also scare you into not making these types of mistakes. For most types of actions that lead to bad credit, the transactions will be on your credit report for seven years. These actions include late payments, any repossessions that have occurred, foreclosures, short sales, and tax liens. The only category that will stay on your credit report longer than seven years is filing for bankruptcy. This type of misdemeanor will remain on your report for an entire decade. Understanding how long your credit history stays with you brings with it an awareness of how important it is to pay your credit off on time.

Step 1: Get Your Credit Report Transcripts

Cleaning up your credit, this first step is to get a copy of your most recent credit report. This report will give you the exact reasons why your credit is in the toilet, and you need to pinpoint what is going on within this report ever to fix it. You don't have to pay any money to obtain these records. Through the Fair Credit and Reporting Agency, you are entitled to receiving a free copy of your credit report once a year. While doing this, it's essential to obtain records from each of the major credit reporting agencies. This way, you will be able to see how each type of credit reported is being perceived by the creditors that you choose. It's impossible to know which credit a potential will use, so you want all of these types of credit reports to be up-to-date.

Step 2: How to Clean Up Your Credit Report

Once you've gotten ahold of your credit reports, it's not enough to simply say, "clean them up." You need to know how to make your credit report look more attractive specifically. Let's take a look at how to do this now.

Tip 1: Finding the Mistakes

It might come as a surprise, but not all of the activity on your credit report is necessarily true. There might be mistakes. If there are, you need to dispute these claims. You will need to dispute this activity with the account that first put these charges on your account. To do this, you can either send a letter to the company in question or call their customer service line. These days, someone should be able to help you at most times during the day.

Tip 2: Dispute the Same Claims on Different Credit Reports

If you find that the same mistakes are apparent on different credit reports that you obtain, you will need to dispute each claim that is listed on the various credit reports. It's not enough to simply dispute one of the applications on one of your credit reports, because these mistakes will still exist on the other reports that have been generated under your name. It can be tedious work, but it's worth it in the end.

Tip 3: Hire an expert

While you may have the money to figure out how to remove potential errors on your credit report on your own, you may not feel like going through the hassle of removing these inaccurate findings on your own. Credit repair companies and law firms do exist that will take care of these banalities for you. These companies are not allowed to promise that they can raise your credit score by any number of points. They will be upfront and honest with you. If they're not and you feel like they're not a trustworthy source, find help elsewhere.

Step 3: Look for Positive Reinforcement

Secured credit cards, are specifically designed to help people who are having credit problems resolve their credit issues. Just because you've been denied certain types of credit because of your past actions, this doesn't mean that you're entirely out of luck. You have a chance to slowly repair your credit with this type of credit card opportunity. As with any card, you will have to develop better habits if you hope to revitalize your credit history.

Step 4: Be Consistent in Your Payment Amounts

It's essential to avoid hinting that you are going through tough times or that you are experiencing financial trouble. To prevent this, it's necessary to, in addition to paying your credit cards off on time, to also pay a consistent amount each month. For example, if you usually spend two hundred dollars each month on your credit card payments, and then suddenly you start to pay fifty dollars or even only twenty-five dollars, your creditors are going to notice. Be consistent in your payments so that your lenders don't worry.

Step 5: Places to Avoid Using a Credit Card

In addition to keeping your risk under control, you should also avoid using your credit card in certain places such as pawnshops or with divorce attorneys. These types of situations indicate that you might soon be in a position of financial stress, and your creditors will deduct your credit score accordingly.

CHAPTER 15:

Use a Credit Card to Build Your Credit Score

Y our credit score is perhaps the most valuable publicly available measure of your financial health. It tells a potential lender or employer briefly just how responsibly (or not) you use credit.

In short, a credit score is a number that depicts a consumer's creditworthiness. Your credit score will be a number ranging from 300-850. From a lender's point of view, the higher your score, and the more attractive a borrower you are.

Who Determines Your Credit Score?

There are several credit scoring systems available. Each one is proprietary to its developing company and uses a somewhat different algorithm to calculate your credit score.

As we will see a little bit later, several factors go into determining your credit score. Each one contributes a certain percentage of the final score you are awarded. It may vary depending on the scoring model used, but the factors tend to remain consistent across all models.

Ultimately, however, it is YOU that determines your credit score. It all comes down to whether you have taken out credit before, and if so, how responsibly you have been using it.

What Credit Scores Are Used For?

Your credit score is a measure of your financial health. It cannot be affected by external parties (save for filling in actual financial information related to you) and is unbiased. Your credit score is personal information and is not available to anybody and everybody that can use Google search. Rest assured that your credit history is not randomly bouncing around the Internet unless you choose to make it publicly available.

Note that if somebody other than you use your personal information to obtain your credit score without your permission, you can take legal action. You can sue for $1000 or actual damages incurred, whichever is greater.

A credit score can, however, be accessed by authorized parties as and when necessary. As such, it can be (and usually is) used by several companies and institutions when deciding whether to offer you their services or not.

Your credit score is checked any time you apply for a loan. It includes everything from student loans to housing and car loans. Potential employers, insurance companies, landlords, and utility companies also have access to this information. So do several government agencies. They may use it to get your contact information, determine if you have unclaimed income, see how much you can afford in child support, and much more.

Your credit score is used to determine how worthy (or truthful) a credit customer you are. Potential lenders and service providers use it to calculate how much of a risk you present to them as a borrower. Legal entities will use it to determine how to act consistently with the laws involved.

How Credit Scores Work

The key to improving your credit score is in understanding what it is made of and how it works. If you can break it down into its components, you can tackle each one separately. It makes it simpler to understand what is coming from where, and how best and quickest to change things for the better.

How Credit Scores Are Created?

There are several different scoring systems available today. Each one has its proprietary algorithm and approaches things differently. Each company or entity chooses which system to use. In a few cases, they may look at your credit score calculated using several methods before deciding.

FICO scores are by far the most used, with over 90% of credit institutions relying on them. Data analytics company FICO (formerly Fair Isaac Corporation) does not reveal its proprietary algorithm used to calculate the final score. But it is known that the formula relies on five major components, each weighted according to importance.

But, as I have already said, FICO's is not the only current score calculation system out there. There are several others. Due to differences in the calculation mechanisms used, your score may differ by as much as 100 points from policy to system.

Commonly Used Scoring Systems

We have already mentioned the FICO score, which is the most widely accepted score calculation method. FICO uses several different scoring models, each designed for a specific purpose. Their NextGen scoring model, for example, is used to assess consumer credit risk, while the FICO SBSS is used to evaluate small businesses applying for credit.

FICO relies on the three national credit bureaus to calculate credit scores. These are Experian, Equifax, and TransUnion. Each of these credit bureaus may have different information on anyone given consumer.

These same three bureaus, in a bid to outcompete FICO, collaborated to produce their credit scoring system. Known as the Vantage Score, it differs from FICO in several ways. A credit report created using the Vantage Score may show significantly different values than one for which FICO was used.

Although not as commonly used as FICO, Vantage Score is also well-accepted by the financial community. Some financial institutions will pull credit reports from both systems for a consumer before deciding.

There are some other scoring systems available too. CE Score is published by CE analytics. Currently, this score is made available to over 6,000 lending institutions across the U.S.

And frequently, financial institutions may choose to use non-traditional credit scores to gain further insight into their consumers. Most of these scores are based on data not available to the national credit bureaus. Such credit scores may rely more on utility, rental, and telecom payment data. Public record information such as mortgages, property deeds, and tax records may also come into play.

Credit Score Values

Each time your credit score is calculated, it will come up with a specific value. The range for these values depends on the scoring system used. FICO and Vantage Score 4.0 (the latest Vantage Score model) both calculate a score ranging from 300 – 850. Other scoring systems have entirely different scoring ranges. In general, though, one thing remains common across all orders: the higher your score, the better for you. While no calculation model is perfect, lending institutions still view consumers with a higher rating as carrying a lower risk. It makes them more likely to offer you their services and gets you a better deal.

As FICO is by far the most used credit score, we will take a closer look at how their credit ranges are broken down. The FICO Score 9 model is the most recent, but many institutions are still using the FICO 8 model, so that is what we will break down below.

FICO Score 8 Ranges and How Lenders View Them

SCORE RANGE	CLASSIFICATION
300-559	Poor
560-669	Fair
670-739	Good
740-799	Very Good
800-850	Excellent

How Credit Scores Are Calculated

What your credit score reads is based on the factors considered when calculating it. These will vary significantly across different scoring systems, and even across different scoring models within the same network.

FICO and Vantage Score, while using different scoring algorithms, both rely on the data from the three national credit bureaus. That is Equifax, Experian, and TransUnion. Other, less traditional scoring systems may use only some of the information available from these three credit bureaus or none. They may choose to rely on data not available from these bureaus, such as rental and utility payment histories. Public record information, such as mortgages, liens, personal property titles, and deeds, is also frequently used.

Each system will use a given set of data to calculate your credit score, assigning each component weight or importance. It usually comes through as each component contributing a specific percentage toward the final score. Some elements, such as your payment history, will weigh very heavily. Other things, like new credit, will have a much lower impact. Again, this varies according to the scoring system used.

CHAPTER 16:

Credit Repair Expectations

Y ou may be asking yourself why so much fuss about credit scores. The simple fact is that most of us are not lucky enough to be millionaires and do not have unlimited liquid capital. It means that we may need to take out loans during our lives, often more than once.

And all of us have our everyday lives to live. We all need access to basics like water, electricity, and telecom, and we all must have somewhere to live. Your credit score is the first thing most of these providers will look at when you apply for their services.

Having a less-than-optimal credit score can hurt you in several measurable ways. The better your score, the better your chances of getting the services you want when you want them, and the less they will cost you in the end.

Getting a Loan

There are times in our lives we make a big, important decision and need financial assistance to see it through. Getting yourself through college will often require taking out a student loan. Buying a car, outfitting your kitchen with appliances, or a big occasion like a wedding may also need a loan. And for most of us, purchasing a house without taking a loan is impossible.

Lending institutions will pull up your credit report before deciding whether to give you a loan or not. A poor credit score (or a sparse credit history) reads as a high-risk customer to these people, resulting in nothing positive for you. They may agree to lend you less than what you requested, or simply reject your proposal altogether.

Interest Rates

The influence of your credit score does not stop with you being able to get a loan or not. Even after the lender has decided to offer you their services, a bad credit score will cost you dearly.

The lower your score, the higher the interest rate on your loan. Again, this is because they view you as a high-risk customer. They may also give you a shorter period within which to repay your loan. Ultimately, these two factors put a more significant financial burden on you.

Employment Opportunities

A well-written resume and customized cover letter can set you apart from the competition and get you through to the interview. You may be professional and charismatic, convincing your future employer that you are the best candidate for the job. What you may not know is that your credit report may then come into play and possibly cost you a brilliant career opportunity.

According to several studies, over 70% of employers carry out background checks on their employees. Some of these will take the time to check your credit report too. This is especially the case for job positions, which need you to handle financial transactions and large sums of money.

Your employer cannot check your credit report without your permission or knowledge. But a bad financial history with several delayed payments or multiple collection accounts can hurt your hiring odds.

Housing

Your credit report also has a direct impact on housing alternatives available to you. Most landlords will insist on checking your credit report before taking you on as a tenant. They want to be sure that you can afford the rent and will be consistent with your payments. A poor credit score may make the landlord reject your application.

Then there is buying a house or apartment. Usually, there is a substantial sum of money involved here, one which most of us cannot afford without a loan. Credit institutions will look at your credit score to determine whether you can afford to service and pay the loan off or not. The score will also learn what interest rate they offer you. The better your score, the less you will ultimately pay.

Insurance

It is not a well-known fact, but your credit score may affect your insurance as well. Your credit health may affect the amount you pay in insurance premiums, be it car insurance, a homeowner's policy, or even health insurance.

Just like lenders, insurance providers are interested in calculating the risk they are taking with you. If your credit score tells them you are irresponsible with your finances, it can send a message that you are careless in other areas of life too.

This makes you a higher insurance liability and will affect the price of your insurance policy. In short, a higher credit score equals lower risk and, therefore, lower premiums.

CHAPTER 17:

Credit Report Sample Dispute Letter

What Is A Credit Report and What is in It?

There is a lot of information on the credit report, and it can vary from person to person and across the credit bureaus. It is because creditors provide different types of data, at different times, and to various reporting agencies.

Also, everyone's credit history is changed (for instance, a garnishment category may exist on one person's report because they had wages garnished, but the group may not even show up for someone who never had a garnishment). Because of this, I go into great detail explaining just about anything that might be found in a report.

For some people, this section can feel overwhelming, trying to figure it out. If that is your case, I recommend that you skip over areas that do not apply to you. And once you are familiar with this section, you can then come back and use it as a reference.

TIP: Credit reports contain information on the most recently reported activity from your creditors. If you recently made a payment and the story does not show the lower balance, it may be due to the creditor not having reported it yet. Very recent refunds may take a few days to record.

Credit reports vary by the agency producing them, but most of them are generally divided into six main sections with variations between the credit bureaus. Yours may have a different order or use different terminology. The six main sections are:

1. Personal Information / Identifying Information / Consumer Statement / Employment

2. Summary

3. Account History / Account Information

4. Public Information / Public Records

5. Inquiries

6. Creditor Contacts

Personal Information / Identifying Information / Consumer Statement / Employment – this section is used to confirm your identity. It contains basic information about you, such as any names you may use, date of birth, current address, previous address, social security number, and employer information. None of this information is used in your credit score calculation but may be used by creditors to verify the information you submitted to them.

This section may also contain your "Consumer Statement." You are allowed to write a statement and ask the credit bureau to add it to your report. It usually explains a negative item on your story to a potential lender or creditor. For example, it may be something like this, "The 2013 Wells Fargo bank account was a shared account with my ex-wife." Your statement has no impact on your credit score.

- Summary Section – this overview section has a categorized list of all your accounts on the credit report. There are nine categories in the summary section:

- Total accounts – the total number of reports on your statement, including both open and closed.

- Public accounts – number of accounts on your credit report listed as "open."

- Private accounts – number of accounts on your credit report listed as "closed."

- Delinquent – number of accounts listed as currently past due.

- Derogatory – number of accounts negatively impacting your credit score.

- Balances – the total amount of debt owed on all open and closed accounts on your credit report.

- Payments – total monthly payment amount you owe on all accounts.

- Public Records – the number of public records listed on your credit report. It would include documents like bankruptcy filings, tax liens, and court judgments.

- Inquiries – number of questions on your credit report from the last 24 months. These inquiries are recorded when a financial institution looks at your data for a credit application. Checking your credit report does not get recorded, nor does it impact your credit score.

- Account History / Account Information – this section has detailed information about your credit accounts. The accounts are split-up into five categories: real estate, installment, revolving, collection, and others.

- Real Estate – first and second mortgages.

- Installment – fixed-term accounts (non-real estate) with regular payments like a car loan.

- Revolving – open term accounts with varying amounts like a credit card.

- Collection – very delinquent accounts that have been transferred to a collection agency, an attorney, or the creditor's internal collections department. They can include foreclosures, repossessions, and reports that have been charged off as well.

- Other – accounts that don't fit in the different categories or their details are unknown. 30 Day accounts like an American Express card may be here.

What is recorded in Each Account?

With each account, the report will list a summary of the terms and details, including the creditor name, account number, condition, balance, type, and pay status.

Creditor Name – the official account name. Because some companies are managed or owned by more giant financial corporations, this may not be the name you expect or write your check. In some cases, especially if it has gone to a collection agency, it may also be nonfinancial institutions such as a library, video rental or Cable Company, or even a cell phone company.

Account Number – the identifying number for your account. Usually, a portion of the name is hidden for security reasons. The report may indicate two numbers if this has gone to a collection agency, one for the collections and one for the original debt.

Condition – according to the most recent update from the creditor, the account will be open, closed, or paid off.

Balance – the amount currently owed on the account. It is based on the last reported activity from the creditor and may not be entirely up to date. If the mind has gone to a collection agency, this will be the amount owed when it was transferred.

Type – common types include credit cards, cars, real estate, and student loans.

Pay Status – payment status according to the most recent update from the creditor. There will also be information about payment history over the past 24 months.

Past Due – the amount of payment overdue based on the most recent reports from the creditors.

High Balance – this is the most you have ever owed on the account. For a house, it would be the initial mortgage amount. For a credit card, it would be the most you ever charged on it.

Terms – this usually applies to loans and the number of payments scheduled. For instance, a 30-year home loan would show a repayment schedule of 360 months (30 years x 12 months).

Limits – the maximum amount you can borrow on this credit account.

Payment – the minimum amount you are required to pay each month.

Opened – the date the account was opened. If the mind has gone to a collection agency, this may be the date it was transferred.

Reported – the last time any activity took place on this account. Recent activity will not show up until it is published by the credit agency.

Responsibility – this is the type of trust you have for this account. For instance, it could be a joint, cosigner, or individual account.

Late Payments – details any late payments you have had over the last seven years.

Remarks – other notes about your account from the creditor. If the report has gone to a collection agency, it may have a statement like "The collection agency has been unable to locate the account holder" or "The account holder has never responded to requests from the collection agency."

TIP: When accounts are unpaid and sent to a collection agency, some of this information may get confusing. For instance, the date may change to the time the collection agency took over, as opposed to when the account was created. The account number may vary, as well. To help with this, some reporting companies like TransUnion will list collection accounts separately.

Public Information / Public Records – this section contains publically available information affecting your credit and is usually limited to legal matters. These may include federal or state tax liens, bankruptcies, and judgments against you in civil cases.

Three types of public records may show up in your credit report: bankruptcies, tax liens, and civil judgments.

- Bankruptcies – a legal filing that appease a person of some or all of their debts. Tax Liens – a claim filed by any government tax agency against a person who they believe owes back taxes. An unpaid tax lien will remain on the credit report for ten years, while a paid tax lien will remain for seven years after the claim is settled.

- Civil Judgments – general category but is usually used to record judgment against you in a civil court.

- Others occasionally, other public information related items may make their way to a credit report. They are rarely reported individually but may show up as part of another public record that gets published, or as part of a remark added to your report by a creditor. They might include:

- Marital Items – could be any legal filing related to a matrimonial or divorce issue.

- Financial Counseling – could be any public record indicating you have received financial counseling.

- Personal Property Liens – this is a type of lien usually filed when a loan is secured against private property.

- Foreclosures – this record indicates a loan was defaulted on, and the creditor has taken over the property.

- Garnishments – a court order to hold back some or all of a person's wages to repay a debt.

CHAPTER 18:

Sample Letter Can Be Used For Debt Collector Stop Call

W hen a lender is considering giving you a loan or a credit card, the lender will contact one of the three credit bureaus for a copy of your credit history. Depending on the information in your file, the lender will decide whether to lend to you and if so, how much and at what interest rate.

When you hear credit reports being discussed, you will usually hear them referred to as "snapshots" of individual finances. While that may be technically accurate to a point, it is also somewhat misleading because credit reports contain far more information about your financial life than what the word "snapshot" implies.

If you have been an adult and running your finances, your credit report will be more than just a page or "snapshot. "Unless you have kept your funds separate from any banks or financial institutions and paid for everything in cash, your credit report will have at least 5-10 pages of unique information about your finances.

The longer you borrow money and interact with financial institutions, the longer your credit report will be. However, a lengthy credit report is not necessarily a bad thing – it is only "bad" for you if it is showing severe money mismanagement, overwhelming debt, and unreliability regarding repayment of debts. Even then, it is not a "bad" thing either – it is simply made up of your facts, your financial actions, and your economic history.

As the saying goes, "knowledge is power," and this is no exception when it comes to your finances. Credit reports contain the most relevant financial information that you need, no matter what season of life you are currently in.

Credit Report Sections

Credit reports typically have five main sections that are personalized with your specific information.

Section 1: Personal Profile

The first section contains your personal information. In addition to identifying information like your name and mailing address, it includes your legal name (or names if you have legally changed your name at any time), your birth year, all addresses on record for your past and present, and also all of the places you have been legally employed since your very first day in the workforce in any arena.

Section 2: Accounts Summary

The summary of your accounts is usually found within the first couple of pages of your credit report and often includes the following information:

• How many accounts are listed negatively

- How many accounts are in collections

- The total amount of real estate debt (home and properties)

- The total amount of debts considered installment loans (e.g., car loans, appliance loans)

- The total amount of revolving debt (e.g., credit cards)

- The percentage of revolving credit available

Section 3: Public Records

This section pertains to any legal "losses," including being the object of a court proceeding, having filed for bankruptcy, or having received judgments or tax liens. This section is left blank of no public records exist.

Section 4: Credit Inquiries

This section lists inquiries made into your credit file by those legally allowed to base on your having given permission. This could include your employer, insurance companies, and lenders like large financial institutions. It would also include any inquiries you have made, by requesting a copy of your credit report, for example.

Section 5: Account History

This contains a list of all your credit accounts, those currently open as well as those that have been closed. This is also where the same creditors will indicate problems with late or missing payments. With so much valuable information, you must look very carefully through the details each time you run your report.

If you find any errors in the numbers, or if there are credit accounts you do not recognize as belonging to you, you need to send a dispute letter immediately to the credit agency, which generated the report as well as to the company, which included the incorrect information.

For each creditor or account on your report, you should see the following specifics documented:

- Creditor Information: The name of the company reporting information about your account.

- Your Account Number: Unique to the company.

- Responsible Parties: The name or names of those responsible for the account, usually using one or more abbreviations:

- I – stands for Individual

- U – stands for Undesignated

- J – stands for Joint

- A – stands for Authorized Owner

- M – stands for Maker

- T – stands for Terminated

- C – stands for Co-maker/Co-signer

- S – stands for Shared

- Opening Date: The year and month, the account was opened with the creditor.

- Creditor Reporting: How many months the creditor has been reporting information concerning the account.

- Last Account Activity: The date of the previous activity of any kind by anyone on the account.

CHAPTER 19:

Use This Letter to Dispute a Debt Collection You're Not Sure

I t sets forth seven essential consumer rights embodied in the Fair Credit Reporting Act. It also provides an understanding of what you can do when those rights have been overlooked, ignored, or willfully trampled by violators.

Consumer Reporting Agencies have been heavily regulated since 1970, and for a good reason. Today in this Information Age, we need the FCRA more than ever!

Because of the free flow of information in our day, the amount of data that CRAs can collect, store, and share about you is more significant than ever before. This information is so valuable that criminals are continually attempting to hack into it—and sometimes they are successful.

With the increase in data collection comes the plague of corrupted data and misreporting of data that can find its way into your consumer files and your consumer reports, which are then shared with users who make decisions that affect you, some examples of which you will read about below. Therefore, you must remain vigilant!

In a nutshell, here is the problem that needs to be prevented or fixed:

Information that is stolen or false information that does not belong in your consumer files and consumer reports can destroy your credit scores—and lead to canceled credit, no credit, higher interest rates, loss of job opportunities, no insurance, or higher insurance premiums. These are devastating consequences—and all it takes is for wrong information to be placed in or remain in your consumer files. Let me share with your real-life examples from lawsuits that have been filed in court that prove the significant consequences caused by violators, and how much jurors dislike these violators.

Loss of employment opportunities. Kevin Mills applied for a position at Starbucks. He was hired, subject to the successful completion of a background investigation by a consumer reporting agency. The background check came back with two convictions for domestic violence. Kevin Mills had never been convicted of domestic violence. He received a call from Starbucks indicating that they would not be hiring him based upon the contents of the consumer report. Later, the story came in the mail, telling him why he had not been appointed. He contacted the consumer reporting agency who provided the information, disputed the data, and they realized that they had made a mistake. Even though the error was cleared up, Starbucks would not reconsider its decision not to hire him. Kevin Wills v. Starbucks Corporation, Active Case, No. 1:17-CV-03654-CAP-CMS.

Loss of Credit. A consumer contacted my office recently. She had accidentally made a partial payment on one of her credit card bills and was short a few dollars. The next month, her credit reports indicated that she had not made any payment. Two weeks later, two banks that had issued her other credit cards canceled their lines of credit.

Loss of Earning Capacity. One of my current clients went to use a credit card to rent a hotel room while working a job out of state. The hotel ran his card and told him it was declined. He called the bank and found out that they said he had recently filed bankruptcy; however, his bankruptcy had been filed more than ten years before that, and he had dismissed the bankruptcy after he had regained employment. He asked for the inaccurate information to be removed, but he was ignored. Because of this, he was denied credit lines that would have allowed him to take on more work. He also had to pay two to three times the regular interest rate to purchase cars for his family members.

Cancellation of Insurance All these problems could have been resolved by applying the laws outlined in the Fair Credit Reporting Act. The FCRA is your key to correcting mistakes on your credit and other consumer reports that can profoundly affect your life. The FCRA is also the tool you use to combat identity theft.

The FCRA can't benefit you to the fullest extent if you don't know what your rights are, and what you must do to exercise them. You must do certain things, or the FCRA does little to benefit you. For example, you need to write letters, complaints, make your case, request information, etc. (For most people, the only way they use the FCRA is to obtain free copies of their credit reports each year.)

Your key to (a) maintaining accurate credit reports, (b) knowing what information each CRA has stored about you that goes into your consumer reports (some of which you generally never see), and (c) protecting your identity, is found in the Fair Credit Reporting Act. To turn that key, you must know what to do and how to do it.

Know Your Rights!

Many consumer protections laws have been passed at both the federal and state levels In 2003, Congress passed the Fair Accounting and Transactions Act (FACTA), which was added to the FCRA. This provided further protection from identity theft and enacted measures that you can take if your identity is stolen. The FCRA contains several consumer rights. You must be proactive in exercising some of them.

Here is a list of your important rights:

A-List of Your Most Important Rights under the FCRA

1. Accuracy. You have the right to expect that before reporting information about you, CRAs will" follow reasonable procedures to assure maximum possible accuracy of the information." See 15 U.S.C. § 1681e (b).
2. Correcting Errors. You have the right to request corrections and deletions to errors noted on your credit reports, consumer reports, and things someone could see that are contained in your consumer files; CRAs and furnishers must both conduct reasonable investigations. See 15 U.S.C. § 1681i and 15 U.S.C. § 1681s-2(b), respectively.

3. Permissible Users. You have the right to sue those who do not have a lawful purpose of obtaining information from your consumer report. See 15 U.S.C. § 1681b.

4. Identity Theft Protection. You have the right to request a credit freeze or credit block to keep users from accessing your consumer files. See 15 U.S.C. § 1681c-1 and 15 U.S.C. § 1681c-2.

5. Full File Disclosure. You have the right to request a full disclosure of everything that is in your consumer files and receive a copy of the same. See 15 U.S.C. § 1681g(a)(2); and

6. Scope of Investigation. You have the right to find out what a CRA did to investigate your request for correction or deletion. 15 U.S.C. § 1681i(a)(6)(B)(iii).

7. The Right to Sue. The FCRA grants you the right to sue a violator of the law.

CHAPTER 20:

How to Write a Letter to Close Your Credit Card

I f you find any errors, here are the two steps that you must take to fix them. The error may be an innocent mistake or a sign of something more serious such as identity theft — both way, and you need to find out and fix it.

1.In writing, inform the credit reporting agency that is showing an error on their report. Unless they consider your request frivolous, they are generally required to investigate within 30 days. To expedite the process, provide them with all the information (copies, not originals!) they could need from you to begin their investigation.

2.In writing, inform the company that provided the inaccurate information to the credit reporting agency that they made an error, and you are formally requesting an investigation. Provide them with all relevant information in your possession that proves the accuracy of your claim. Again, send copies, not originals, of any documentation that you provide.

Expert Tip #1: Even if a credit reporting agency allows you to report an issue via telephone, this may not be your best option. Ideally, you ought to have copies of all correspondence so that you can refer to them if things get lost. Make photocopies of all written communication, save copies of any e-mails that you send, and take screenshots of any information you provide via online Contact Us forms.

To take a screenshot on a PC, press and hold the Alt button while you press the Print Screen key. The Print Screen key is located near the upper-right corner of your keyboard.

Expert Tip #2: When mailing documentation, pay extra for the service that provides you with proof of delivery. This way, you will be 100% certain that the information was received promptly.

If you win your claim, the company that reported the inaccurate information must inform all three major credit bureaus of the error. In addition to that, the credit reporting agency whose report showed the error must provide you a corrected copy of your credit report for free.

Once the credit reporting agency agrees to correct the error, it could take a few weeks for the change to show up. If you require the correction to occur sooner to facilitate your approval for a loan, ask your lender about a rapid rescore. This service is not available directly to consumers, but to lenders — it often allows for credit scores to be corrected within days.

So, say you are applying for a mortgage, and correcting an error could lead to an increase in your score and a better interest rate for your mortgage. If you can provide your lender with proof of the failure, they may be able to expedite a rapid rescore for you (extra fees may apply).

However, there are no guarantees that you'll be granted a rapid rescore, so the best option is to check over your credit reports a few months in advance and allow lots of time for any errors to be investigated and corrected.

5 Bonus Tips

1. If you are checking your credit report to verify accuracy before obtaining credit, be sure to ask the creditor which report and score system they use so you can check those first. You might as well start with the essential credit reports.

2. If you are like most people, checking each of your three credit reports once a year will be plenty to keep on top of things. As for your actual credit score, according to FICO, in three months, 75% of people have a change in their credit score of fewer than 20 points — in other words, for most people, the month-to-month changes in their credit scores are relatively small. So, it is probably not worth paying for access to your credit score too often unless you need to know your number to check double what kind of shape, you're in.

3. Generally speaking, collection accounts should be removed from your credit report after seven years. If you see any older than that, contact the relevant credit reporting agency and ask if it can be removed.

4. Don't worry if you see a bunch of "Account Management" or "Account Maintenance" inquiries from your credit card company — it is perfectly normal for them to check your credit reports periodically, and these checks will not affect your credit score.

5. To check up on your FICO score, look at my FICO report — it will even tell you what negative factors might be affecting your score.

CHAPTER 21:

Need to Send a Pay For The Letter Delete? Use This Easy Model

Pay off what you owe: While this is going to be easier said than done in most situations, according to Experian, the ideal amount of credit utilization that you want is 30 percent or less. While there are other ways to increase your credit utilization rating, paying off what you owe on time each month will also go towards showing you can pay your bills on time, essentially pulling double duty when it comes to improving your credit score. It will also make it easier to follow through on the following tips.

Pay your credit card bills twice a month: If you have a credit card that you use regularly, say for example because it offers you reward points, so much so that you max it out each month, it may be hurting your credit even though you pay it off in full at the end of each month. This may be the case due to the way the credit card company reports to the credit bureau; depending on when they say each month, it could show that your credit utilization rate is close to 100 percent depending on what your credit line currently is, thus hurting your credit score. As such, paying off your credit card in two smaller chunks throughout the month can help boost your credit without costing you anything extra overall.

Increase your credit limit: If you aren't currently in a position to pay down your credit card balance, you can still improve your credit utilization rate by increasing your current credit limit. It is an easy way to improve your credit utilization rate without putting any more money out upfront. If you do this, however, you mustn't take advantage of the increased credit line as if you find yourself up against the limit again, you will be worse off than when you started. Only pursue this option if you have the willpower to avoid racking up extra charges, especially if you are already strapped when it comes to the payments you need to make each month; decreasing your credit utilization limit while also creating more late payments is a lateral move at best.

Open a new account: Improving your credit utilization rate is one of the best ways to start rebuilding your credit. If your current credit card company doesn't increase your credit limit, you may way to try applying for another credit card instead. If your loan is not so hot, then your rates are going to be higher, but this won't matter as long as you don't plan on using the card in the first place. Remember, the credit utilization rate is a combination of your total available lines of credit, so this can be an excellent way to drop your current utilization rate substantially, especially if you won't be able to pay off what you currently owe for a significant period.

Keep in mind, however, that if you choose this route, then you are only going to want to apply for one new card every couple of months, especially if you aren't sure if you are going to be approved, as too many hard credit inquiries will only cause your credit score to drop, even if you do end up with a better credit utilization rate as a result. Spreading out these requests will give the inquiries time to drop off naturally and will prevent you from looking desperate to potential lenders, which can also make it more challenging to get a new card.

Authorized users: If you don't have the credit to get a new credit card, or even to extend your current credit line, then your best choice may be to find someone you trust and ask them to become an authorized user on their card. While most people will likely balk at the idea, you may be able to appease them by explaining that you don't need a copy of their card or have any intent on using it, simply being listed on the map is enough to improve your credit utilization rating. Not only that, but you will also get credit for the on-time payments that this other person makes as well.

CHAPTER 22:

Sample Letter to Be Sent To Deb Collectors on a Debt That Has Expired

Identity theft is a current crisis in the US that is continuing to grow every year. An Identity Theft Resource Center (ITRC) report is quite disturbing. It shows that 1,579 data breaches exposed about 179 million identity records in 2017.

It will be a lot of problem to you if you will be a victim of an identity scam. Downfall of your credit score would be the worst case

How identity theft can ruin your credit score

The most common type of identity theft crime is credit card fraud. Fraudsters would steal your personal information and your credit card details. They would then use the stolen information for unauthorized transactions.

The fraudsters can either steal your credit card or perform a card-not-present fraud. But they would also need information such as your birthday and Social Security number.

You may end up with a credit card bill that you might not be able to pay or handle if you become a victim. This may affect your credit score if you do not act on it fast.

Ways to avoid becoming an identity theft victim

Proving that you are a victim of identity theft can be inconvenient. There is a long process to go through, which involves a lot of documentation before you can prove your innocence.

It would still be best to avoid these kinds of troubles, and there are several ways you can do it.

1. Watch out for Phishing Scams

A phishing scam is a criminal's method to get personal information such as passwords. The most common way of phishing is sent via e-mail.

These e-mails would look like official e-mails from a bank or other companies. The contents would often inform you about system changes or promotional offers. It would ask you to enter personal information because of these reasons. In some cases, these emails scare you into providing info by saying that that access to your account will be restricted if you do not "update" your account.

The e-mail would also contain an external link to a fraud web page that would look like the bank's legit website. Entering your details on this page will result in significant problems for you. The criminals will use your features to perform transactions under your name.

You can avoid being a victim by remembering one fundamental rule: Banks generally will never ask for your information. If you must make sure you need to update your account, contact your bank first.

To avoid these scams, stay updated with the latest phishing scam techniques. An updated browser and firewalls also help to prevent phishing scams.

There are also anti-phishing toolbars available online. These will alert you if you visit a suspicious website.

2. Protect your computer data

Defrauders can also get vital information about you by hacking your personal computer.

They can use a keylogger that records everything you type on your computer. They may also intercept your Internet traffic and record the information you send online.

People who transact online are the most vulnerable to these kinds of attacks. But there are various ways to safeguard your computer data from hackers.

You must use a firewall and set a password for your Wi-Fi. You should also install reliable anti-malware software. Many hackers use malware and other viruses to get information from computers.

Also, make sure that you are using secured connections. Public Wi-Fi connections are not guaranteed, so it is best to avoid using them as much as possible.

3. Protect your passwords

Using passwords is one of the ways that keep accounts safe. But, not using them properly would still make you vulnerable to identity theft.

Your password must be strong and not guessable. Shocking as it may seem, many people use "password" and "123456" as their passwords. These are the weakest passwords anybody could use.

Avoid using birthdays, phone numbers, or other personal information as your password. It's best to use a combination of numbers, letters, and symbols. In this way, your password will be difficult to crack.

However, highly skilled hackers may still be able to get your password. Using multi-factor authentication, especially for online banking, might add security to your accounts. Some banks, for example, require that you confirm a transaction by using a temporary pin sent to your registered phone number.

You must also have different passwords for different accounts. If one of your accounts gets hacked, all your other accounts would likely be vulnerable as well.

The most important thing to remember is never to share your passwords with anybody.

4. Protect your mail

Imagine all the information an identity thief could get from your mailbox.

Criminals do not only steal information online. They can also get your personal information from the mail you receive if they find a chance.

To avoid mail identity theft, start by cutting down the amount of junk mail you receive. This includes insurance and credit offers.

You should also keep mail with valuable information in a locked container. If your letter is piling up, you can shred them instead.

For incoming mail, you can either get a locking mailbox or a P.O. Box. The locking mailbox looks like a standard mailbox, but it can only be opened with a key—a P.O. Box may be safer than a locking mailbox, but you will need to pay for it monthly.

For outgoing mail, you must avoid putting it in a mailbox, mainly if it contains checks or cash. Instead, drop it off at the post office or in a collection box. You may also hand it directly to a mail carrier.

But with today's technology, companies now offer paperless bills. This will not only prevent mail fraud, but you may also get some small bill discounts.

5. Protect your credit card number

As mentioned above, fraudsters can use your credit card to perform unauthorized purchases. All they need is your credit card number and your personal information.

The basics of securing your credit card start with your signature. Sign the back of your credit card as soon as you get it. Also, do not write and keep your pin in the same place where your card is.

Keep your credit card safe by not letting anyone in public see it. Sometimes, you may receive calls from your "bank." Unless you made the call, never give your card information.

You must also watch out for phishing scam e-mails from your bank. Even if it looks legit, don't give your details or credit card number.

It's also a good idea to update your bank information regularly. Update your phone numbers and e-mail address as soon as changes occur. Also, be up to date with fraud alert systems and respond immediately to notifications.

Lastly, report lost credit cards, or any fraud activity suspicions right away. Your bank can block your account and credit card to avoid others using it.

6. Spot unauthorized credit card charges quickly

It's essential to check your credit card statements regularly. Many unauthorized charges can go unnoticed for months if you do not do this.

Review your statements early and check for any purchases that you did not make. If you do not report it ASAP, your credit card issuer will not give you much time to dispute. Also, you might end up being liable for the charges.

Call your issuer immediately once you spot an unauthorized charge on your account.

Once your credit score is tainted with a bad record, it is difficult to fix it. You may need to endure a negative credit score for some time before you can recover from it. Protect your personal information and educate yourself about the new scam's criminals develop. Always remember that these criminals will never stop finding ways to get what they want.

We do not live in a perfect, crime-free world. You must always be vigilant to protect your interests. You do not have to fall victim to identity theft.

CHAPTER 23:

Disputes Letter for Billing Error

W hen you have gotten an opportunity to fix your credit, there are a few moves you can make to keep up your sound credit. By keeping your credit status reliable, you will have more open doors for low financing costs, and advance and credit card endorsements.

Cutoff the number of hard requests: Soft requests do not affect your credit, like when you mind your credit score. Hard applications can influence your score — and happen when you apply for an advance or new credit card. An excessive number of hard requests in a brief timeframe, for example, two or three months can cause you to appear to be more hazardous and, in this way, can adversely affect your score.

Set up auto-installments: Whether you are paying the full equalization or making a base installment, ensure your payments are on schedule. Sign in online to your credit card, advance and utility records to set up programmed installments. This guarantees you pay on schedule and gives you one less thing to stress over.

Keep old records open: Even on the off chance that you do not utilize a specific credit card all the time yet have had the registration open for some time, do not close it. More established records show that you have kept up a solid installment history with creditors — causing you to show up increasingly creditworthy.

Focus on a blend: Maintaining a combination of various kinds of credit can give your score a lift, for example, paying on a vehicle advance, credit card, and home loan at the same time.

Simply be sure you can make convenient installments before opening new records or obtaining extra cash.

Screen your credit report: Review your credit report, in any event, two times every year to guarantee there are no other blunders.

Discovering mistakes and questioning them can tremendously affect your credit score and your overall capacity to get affirmed by moneylenders.

Stay away from different new records without a moment's delay: While once in a while unavoidable — like if you have to purchase a vehicle simultaneously as applying for a credit card — it's ideal to confine opening a few records inside a brief period. A few creditors see different new files as unsafe. The original documents can likewise bring down your credit age.

Request proficient assistance: If you need to improve your credit standing significantly —

at last prompting endorsement for more enormous advances with better terms — think about asking an expert. You can dramatically enhance your money related remaining with the correct assistance.

CHAPTER 24:

Refusal of Credit Card Interest Rate Increases

Sample Letter for Disputing Errors on Your Credit Report

[Your Name]

[Your Address]

[Your City, State, Zip Code]

[Date]

Complaint Department

[Company Name]

[Street Address]

[City, State, Zip Code]

Dear Sir or Madam:

I am writing to dispute the following information in my file. I have circled the items I dispute on the attached copy of the report I received.

This item [identify the item(s) disputed by the name of the source, such as creditors or tax court, and identify the type of question, such as credit account, judgment, etc.] is [inaccurate or incomplete] because [describe what is incorrect or incomplete and why]. I am requesting that the item be removed [or request another specific change] to correct the information.

Enclosed are copies of [use this sentence if applicable and describe any enclosed documentation, such as payment records and court documents] supporting my position. Please reinvestigate this [these] matter[s] and [delete or correct] the disputed item[s] as soon as possible.

Sincerely,

Your name

Sample Letter for Closing Your Credit Card

Date

Your Name

Address

City, State Zip

Name of Creditor

Address

City, State Zip Code

Re: Account Number: Account Number (or Last Four)

Dear Sir or Madam:

On 6/15/18, I requested by telephone to have my account closed. This letter confirms that request. Any updates to my credit report should reflect the account was closed at my request.

Please send confirmation the account was closed.

Sincerely,

Your Name

Sample Credit Card Billing Dispute Letter

Date

Your Name

Address

City, State Zip

Creditor's Name

Address

City, State Zip

Re: Account Number

Dear Sir or Madam:

This letter is to dispute a billing error on my account in the amount of

$_____. The amount is inaccurate because <describe in detail

why the amount is wrong, e.g., the merchandise was returned, the late fee is incorrect, etc.>.

I have enclosed copies of <describe any enclosed documentation, e.g., return receipt, canceled check, etc. to support my claim. Please correct this billing error as soon as possible.

Sincerely,

Your Name

Sample Pay for Delete Letter

Your Name

Your Address Your City, State Zip

Collector's Name

Collector's Address

Collector's City, State Zip

Date

Re: Account Number XXXX-XXXX-XXXX-XXXX

Dear Collection Manager:

This letter is in response to your [letter/call/credit report entry] on [date] related to the debt referenced above. I wish to save us both some time and effort by settling this debt.

Please be aware that this is not an acknowledgment or acceptance of the debt, as I have not received any verification of the mortgage. Nor is this a promise to pay and is not a payment agreement unless you respond as detailed below.

I am aware that your company can report this debt to the credit bureaus as you deem necessary. Furthermore, you can change the listing since you are the information furnisher.

I am willing to pay [this debt in full / $XXX as settlement for this debt] in return for your agreement to remove all information regarding this debt from the credit reporting agencies within ten calendar days of payment. If you agree to the terms, I will send certified payment in the amount of $XXX payable to [Collection Agency] in exchange to have all information related to this debt removed from all of my credit files.

If you accept this offer, you also agree not to discuss the proposal with any third-party, excluding the original creditor. If you receive the offer, please prepare a letter on your company letterhead agreeing to the terms. This letter should be signed by an authorized agent of [Collection Agency]. The message will be treated as a contract and subject to the laws of my state.

As granted by the Fair Debt Collection Practices Act, I have the right to dispute this alleged debt. If I do not receive your postmarked response within 15 days, I will withdraw the offer and request full verification of this debt.

Please forward your agreement to the address listed above.

Sincerely,

Your Name

Sample Opt-Out Letter for Interest Rate Hikes

Your address

City, state, ZIP code

Today's Date Name of a credit card issuer

Address

City, state, ZIP code

Re: Account number (place your credit card account number here) To whom it may concern:

I have received your notice of change in terms of the above credit card account. The notice gives me until (DATE) to notify (name of a credit card issuer) of my intention to opt-out or reject the increase in my interest rate.

I am rejecting this change in terms and wish to continue to pay the balance of my account under the old terms. I understand that I can no longer use this account. If I use it, the new higher APR will apply to the account.

Please notify me in writing of receipt of this written request to opt-out of the interest rate hikes.

Sincerely,

(Your name as it appears on your account)

Sample Cease and Desist Letter

Date

Your Name

Address

City, State Zip

Debt Collector's Name

Address

City, State Zip

Re: Account Number

Dear Debt Collector:

According to my rights under federal debt collection laws, I am requesting that you cease communication with me, as well as my family and friends, concerning this and all other alleged debts you claim I owe.

You are with this notified that if you do not comply with this request, I will immediately file a complaint with the Federal Trade Commission and the [your state here] Attorney General's office. Civil and criminal claims will be pursued.

Sincerely,

Your Name

Letter To Dispute A Debt Collection You Are Not Sure.

[Your Name]

[Your Address]

[Your City, State, Zip Code]

[Date]

[Collection Company Name]

[Street Address]

[City, State, Zip Code]

I was notified by your company on [date of contact] regarding an alleged debt. I have reason to believe I do not owe this debt because [briefly explain the reason but provide minimal personal info (ex.: "because I have never had an account with that store," or "because I believe you have me confused with a different person," or "because the alleged debt is so old I no longer owe it under state law.")]

I request all the following information be provided to me by mail:

1. The amount of the alleged debt.

2. The full name and mailing address of the original creditor for this suspected debt.

3. Documentation showing you have verified that I am responsible for this debt, or a copy of any judgment.

4. Documentation showing you are licensed to collect debts in [my state].

Because I am writing to you within 30 days of being notified by your company about this debt, you must cease attempting to collect this alleged debt until after you have provided the requested information.

If you continue attempting to collect on this debt — or seek judgment for payment of the debt — without first providing written verification, you will violate the Fair Debt Collection Practices Act. Additionally, the liability cannot accrue any fees or interest beyond what is allowed by state law or by contract with the original creditor.

Sincerely,

[SIGNATURE]

[Your name]

Sample Debt Validation Letter

Today's Date

Your Name

Your Address

Collector's Name

Collector's Address

RE: [insert account number or name of account or name of debt]:

Dear [insert collector's name or company name],

This letter is in response to your [letter dated xx-xx-2005] (copy enclosed) or [phone call on xx-xx-2005], concerning the collection of the above referenced [account or date].

I do not believe I owe what you say I owe; therefore, I dispute this debt. I am well aware of my rights under the Fair Debt Collection Practices Act (FDCPA) and my state laws, so I hope to save both of us a great deal of time by letting you know that not only do I dispute the validity of this debt, I have also checked with my State Attorney General and verified that the Statute of Limitations for enforcing this type of debt through the courts in (insert your state or the state in which the contract was signed) has expired. Therefore, should you decide to pursue this matter in court, I intend to inform the court of my dispute of this debt and that the "statute of limitations" has expired.

This letter is your formal notification that I consider this matter closed and demand that you, or anyone affiliated with your company, stop contacting me by phone on any number regarding this or any other topic. You may contact me in writing to advise me that your debt collection efforts are being terminated or that you or the creditor are taking specific actions allowed by the FDCPA or my state laws.

Be advised that I consider any contact not under the Fair Debt Collection Practices Act a severe violation of the law and will immediately report any violations to my State Attorney General, to the Federal Trade Commission, and, if necessary, take whatever legal action is needed to protect myself. Be advised that I reserve the right to record all phone calls, and violations of the FDCPA can result in you or your company being fined up to $1,000 or more.

(Sign above name)

Printed Name

Conclusions

I n the times we live in, it is almost impossible to live without having at least one credit. The unstable rates of unemployment can affect everyone, which is why more and more Americans are confronted with the problem of bad credit. The unfortunate fact is that more and more people choose to do nothing about it and live with bad credit for a long time. What you have to understand is that bad credit gets even worse over time as its grave consequences will be felt more and more, leading to things such as the impossibility of getting new confidence, refinance an old credit, rent an apartment or get a job. Therefore, you should act in time and take care of your finances, especially in the context of a shaky national and international economy.

Fixing your credit is the best solution and should become more popular in the United States because I think it can really make a difference for a significant number of people. Credit repair might seem complicated to some, and it takes time to finalize, but nothing great is ever accomplished without a little bit of work. Also, no specialist can claim that a credit repair done in one way or another has a one hundred percent success rate. If they do, be careful with people trying to scam you for money while claiming they are repairing your bad credit.

The benefits of fixing your credit might reveal themselves over an extended period, but by carefully doing all the steps, you will eventually clear your confidence and increase your chances of you ending up with increased scores on a credit application. It will also help you with finding a job, even though your credit is not entirely repaired. When someone is evaluating your credit report and sees the written statements and all the work you have put in for the process, it shows how responsible and preoccupied you are about your finances and says a lot about who you are.

Remember to be consistent and make sure to rid yourself of all the unnecessary expenses that you have. Try to establish a new and fresh way to keep track of your payments. Do not be afraid to act, for it is only then that you will be able to see the result. Always think positive, and do not let failure hold you back from your goal to be creditworthy once again. In the end, all the efforts are truly worth it. Not only will you have peace of mind and feel better about your life, but the more important goal is to have a trouble-free process in acquiring a new house or car because of your good and trustworthy credit. What is more, because of that good credit standing, you might even land the job or start the business that you have been dreaming of. Isn't that something to look forward to?

Many people become enthusiastic about credit repairing, and when they see the effort involved and the time required on the journey to excellent credit, they get discouraged and give up. Others give up after the first negative response from a creditor or credit report agency, and some even go through with it but stop doing things to improve their credit when they've finished the process and still haven't managed to fix all the negative items. Damage control is just as important as the process itself, and, as I have said in this subject, it has many future benefits. The important thing about the whole process is to stay motivated and continue improving.

Make sure that you are paying attention to your credit. It is going to be extremely important throughout your life so that you can have fun and do the things you enjoy. To make the most of it, just make sure that you are following and contacting a professional if you continue to have problems with your ability to stay on track and budget.